OXFORD

Spiders

Rose Impey

St. Vincent's Catholic Primary School
Orchard Road
Altrincham
Cheshire
WA15 8EY

OXFORD
UNIVERSITY PRESS

This book belongs to:

OXFORD
UNIVERSITY PRESS

Great Clarendon Street, Oxford OX2 6DP
Oxford University Press is a department of the University of Oxford.
It furthers the University's objective of excellence in research, scholarship,
and education by publishing worldwide in

Oxford   New York

Auckland   Cape Town   Dar es Salaam   Hong Kong   Karachi
Kuala Lumpur   Madrid   Melbourne   Mexico City   Nairobi
New Delhi   Shanghai   Taipei   Toronto

With offices in

Argentina   Austria   Brazil   Chile   Czech Republic   France   Greece
Guatemala   Hungary   Italy   Japan   Poland   Portugal   Singapore
South Korea   Switzerland   Thailand   Turkey   Ukraine   Vietnam

Oxford is a registered trade mark of Oxford University Press
in the UK and in certain other countries

Text © Rose Impey
Illustrations © David Wright
The moral rights of the author have been asserted

Database right Oxford University Press (maker)

This edition 2009

British Library Cataloguing in Publication Data

Data available

ISBN: 978-0-19-911933-2

1 3 5 7 9 10 8 6 4 2

Printed in China
Paper used in the production of this book is a natural,
recyclable product made from wood grown in sustainable forests.
The manufacturing process conforms to the environmental
regulations of the country of origin.

Contents

▶ The hunters

Suddenly the spider is there.
It comes from nowhere, creeping
like a cat, without a sound.
Then – the spider jumps!

It holds the fly with its legs and
stabs with its fangs. The venom
works quickly.

house fly

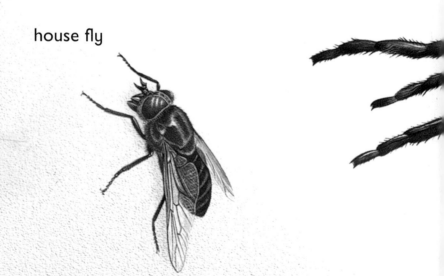

The fly stops struggling; it is paralysed. Now it is ready to eat, the spider sucks it dry.

The jumping spider doesn't make a web. With eight good eyes and eight strong legs, the jumping spider is a great hunter.

jumping spider
salticus scenicus

▶ The Trappers

In the dead of night a beetle walks
the forest floor. The trapdoor spider
hides in its burrow. It knows the
beetle is coming.

Around the burrow are silk trip lines.
The spider feels the lines vibrate.
The beetle comes closer... and closer.

trapdoor spider
liphistius desultor

Pop! The trapdoor opens.

Out darts the spider. It grabs the beetle and pulls it underground.

Pop! The lid closes.

Trapdoor spiders don't need good eyesight. They can feel their prey coming. Trapdoor spiders are great hunters too. They don't make webs either.

The web-builders

All spiders make silk but only a half of all spiders make webs.

The best-known web is the orb web. In any garden you will find dozens of orb webs or a garden spider busy making one.

First the spider makes a silk thread. She draws it out of her spinnerets like liquid silk, but it soon hardens.

Then she begins to build.

garden spider
araneus diadematus

legs

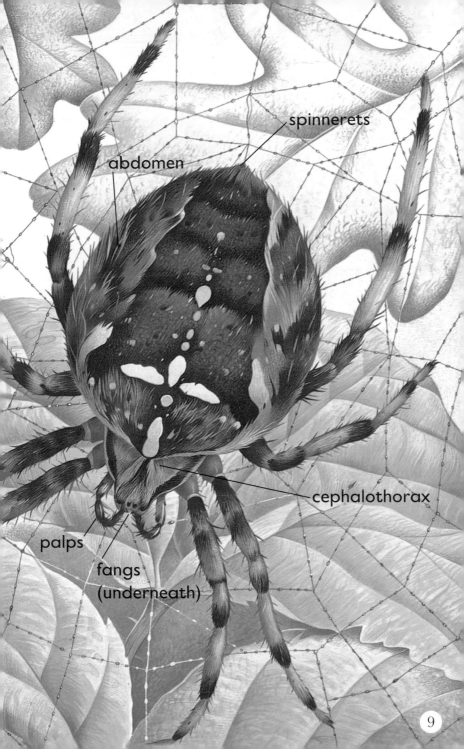

spinnerets

abdomen

cephalothorax

palps

fangs
(underneath)

The spider fixes one end of the thread to a branch. The wind carries her to another nearby. Now she has a bridge.

She crawls back along it with a second thread, then drops down. Now she has a Y shape.

Back and to she travels from the centre making spokes, like a wheel.

She joins them up in a spiral pattern. In one hour she will have a perfect web ready to catch her prey.

▶ All sorts of webs

There are many different kinds of web. The hammock web spider hangs beneath her web, waiting for the insect to fall in.

hammock web spider
linyphia triangularis

Sheet webs have a funnel where the spider hides. Above there's a tangle of sticky threads ready to catch the insect.

Then the spider rushes out… and grabs it!

sheet web with
tegenaria domestica

purse web

Purse web spiders hide inside a silk tube, waiting for the insect to walk across it. Then she grabs it!

purse web spider
atypus affinis

Most webs are made by female spiders. Female spiders are bigger than males, sometimes twenty times bigger! So the male has to be very careful when he comes to mate. He might get eaten by mistake!

▶ Making spiderlings

The male garden
spider fixes a thread
to the female's web.
He pulls it gently,
like ringing
a doorbell.

garden spider
*araneus
diadematus*

When the male wolf spider meets a
female, he waves his legs in the air.

wolf spider
*pardosa
amentata*

The male
jumping spider
does a little
sideways dance.

jumping spider
salticus scenicus

nursery web spider
pisaura mirabilis

The male
nursery web
spider brings
a gift, perhaps
a tasty fly
wrapped in silk.

But sometimes,
if the female
is hungry, the
male still gets
eaten!

▶ Supermums

Spiders make very good mothers. The female lays her eggs in an egg sac wrapped in a silk cocoon.

a spider's egg sac

The nursery web spider spins a silk tent. Her babies live inside the little nursery until they're big enough to leave and find food for themselves.

nursery web spider's tent *pisaura mirabilis*

wolf spider and her babies
pardosa amentata

The wolf spider is a supermum!
She carries her egg sac with her,
stuck to her spinnerets. When the
eggs hatch out she carries her babies
on her back too.

▶ Leaving home

Some spiders only lay two eggs at a time; some garden spiders lay 1,000. In spring the eggs begin to hatch. There are so many the spiderlings may soon start to eat each other. If they want to survive they must escape.

They spin their first silk threads and the wind carries them like little parachutes. 1,000 eggs may hatch but soon many babies will be eaten.

Did you know...
some nephila spiders can produce 1,000 eggs in ten minutes?

Lizards, birds, frogs, toads and shrews, even some insects like wasps and beetles, eat spiders. But enough spiders survive. It is thought that on a summer's day there may be 2 million in a field of grass.

▶ All over the world

Wherever you go in the world you will find spiders: in jungles, swamps, deserts, beaches, deep caves and coal mines, on top of mountains, under Arctic snow.

Some spiders even live in lakes and ponds. The swamp spider is so light it can walk on water. It sits on a leaf dangling its feet, fishing for insects or tadpoles.

swamp spider
dolomedes fimbriatus

water spider
argyroneta
aquatica

The water spider spins a silk web under the water. It ties it to a plant and fills it with a bubble of air. It lives inside its underwater web, swimming out to catch food, like tadpoles and water insects.

▶ A closer look at spiders

insect

spider

Spiders aren't insects. Spiders belong to the arachnid family. Insects have six legs and three parts to their bodies. Spiders have eight legs and two parts. They also have two fangs which they use to bite their prey and inject them with venom.

Most are small and hunt insects. Some are so small you'd need a magnifying glass to see them.

Tiny house spider *oonops domesticus*

Some spiders are so big they'd cover a dinner plate. The bigger ones can eat mice, birds, frogs, even lizards and snakes. But spiders hardly ever bite people.

Mexican red knee tarantula
brachypelma smithi

▶ Scared of spiders?

In fact, spiders help humans by eating pests that carry germs and disease. Yet many people are afraid of spiders. Why is that? Is it because they move quickly? Is it because they appear without a sound? Is it because they have so many long hairy legs?

Mexican blond tarantula
aphonopelma chalcodes

black widow spider
latrodectus mactans

Australian funnel web spider
atrax robustus

We call all large hairy spiders
tarantulas. Most people are afraid of
tarantulas but even their bite doesn't
often kill. The black widow spider
can kill. So can the Australian funnel
web spider.

But most spiders are harmless.
They only hunt for food to stay alive.
Sometimes spiders are hunted too.

Spiders for supper

The Piaroa Indians hunt the giant tarantula. They coax it out of its hole. Then they pounce! They hold it with their thumbs. They stab it with a wooden spike. The spider stops struggling. It is dead.

Did you know...
the biggest spider in the world lives in the Amazon Forest of South America? It is the size of a large dinner plate.

The Indians wrap it in leaves, like a parcel, all wrapped up and ready to cook. They cook the spider in a fire. They think it is delicious. The Piaroa Indian hunts for his food. Just like the spider. They are both great hunters.

giant tarantula
theraphosa blondi

▶ Glossary

 abdomen The abdomen of a spider is the main part of her body. **9**

 cephalothorax The head and the part joining the head to the abdomen of a spider. **9**

 cocoon A cocoon is a silk case the spider wraps her egg sac in to protect it. **16**

 egg sac An egg sac is a silk bag in which the spider keeps her eggs. **16, 17**

 fangs Fangs are the sharp claws on the spider's head which it uses to bite its prey and poison it. **4, 9, 24**

mate When a male and female spider join up to make babies, it is called mating.   **13**

palps Palps are feelers which a spider uses to touch and test things when looking for food. **9**

prey An animal that is hunted by another animal for food is called its prey.   **7, 11, 24**

spiderlings Spiderlings are baby spiders.   **14, 18**

spinnerets The openings at the tip of a spider's abdomen from which it draws out silk.

8, 9, 17

OXFORD

WILD READS

WILD READS will help your child develop a love of reading and a lasting curiosity about our world. See the websites and places to visit below to learn more about spiders.

Spiders

WEBSITES

http://www.bbc.co.uk/cbbc/wild/extremeanimals/

http://www.uksafari.com/spiders.htm

http://www.tooter4kids.com/Spiders/Spiders.htm

PLACES TO VISIT

Some people find spiders very scary but there are no dangerous spiders in the UK. Look out for spiders in your own home and garden or any other outdoor spaces.

Other places where you can see more exotic and dangerous spiders in a safe environment:

Whipsnade Zoo
http://www.zsl.org/zsl-whipsnade-zoo/

Chester Zoo
http://www.chesterzoo.org/

London Zoo
http://www.zsl.org/